Sous V

Recipes at Home

Discover New Techniques and Cook Amazing Dishes with Simple and Mouthwatering Recipes. Step by Step Cookbook.

Marielle Sanford

The following Book is reproduced below with the goal of providing information that is as accurate and reliable as possible. Regardless, purchasing this Book can be seen as consent to the fact that both the publisher and the author of this book are in no way experts on the topics discussed within and that any recommendations or suggestions that are made herein are for entertainment purposes only. Professionals should be consulted as needed prior to undertaking any of the action endorsed herein.

This declaration is deemed fair and valid by both the American Bar Association and the Committee of Publishers Association and is legally binding throughout the United States.

Furthermore, the transmission, duplication, or reproduction of any of the following work including specific information will be considered an illegal act irrespective of if it is done electronically or in print. This extends to creating a secondary or tertiary copy of the work or a recorded copy and is only allowed with the express written consent from the Publisher. All additional right reserved.

The information in the following pages is broadly considered a truthful and accurate account of facts and as such, any inattention, use, or misuse of the information in question by the reader will render any resulting actions solely under their purview. There are no scenarios in which the publisher or the original author of this work can be in any fashion deemed liable for any hardship or damages that may befall them after undertaking information described herein.

Additionally, the information in the following pages is intended only for informational purposes and should thus be thought of as universal. As befitting its nature, it is presented without assurance regarding its prolonged validity or interim quality. Trademarks that are mentioned are done without written consent and can in no way be considered an endorsement from the trademark holder.

Table of Contents

BREAKFAST

Cinnamon Rice Pudding

Preparation time: 10 minutes

Cooking time: 40 minutes

Servings: 4

Ingredients:

1 teaspoon cinnamon powder

½ teaspoon vanilla extract

1 cup white rice

2 cups almond milk

3 tablespoons sugar

Directions:

In a sous vide pouch, mix the rice with the milk and the other ingredients, whisk, seal, submerge in your sous vide machine and cook at 180 degrees F for 40 minutes.

Divide the rice pudding into bowls and serve.

Nutrition: calories 141 fat 2 fiber 6 carbs 7 protein 5

Spinach and Eggs Mix with Asparagus

Preparation time: 10 minutes

Cooking time: 50 minutes

Servings: 4

Ingredients:

- Cooking spray
- 1 teaspoon smoked paprika
- Salt and black pepper to the taste
- 1 teaspoon chives, chopped
- 2 asparagus spears, chopped
- 4 eggs whisked
- ¼ cup parmesan, grated
- ½ cup heavy cream

Directions:

Grease 4 ramekins with the cooking spray, and divide the eggs mixed with the asparagus and the other ingredients in each.

Preheat your water oven, place ramekins inside, cover them with tin foil and cook everything at 180 degrees F for 50 minutes.

Serve for breakfast.

Nutrition: calories 211 fat 3 fiber 6 carbs 8 protein 5

Coconut Eggs

Preparation time: 10 minutes

Cooking time: 40 minutes

Servings: 4

Ingredients:

½ teaspoon nutmeg, ground

3 tablespoons sugar

2 tablespoons coconut milk

4 eggs, whisked

1 cup coconut cream

Directions:

In a bowl, mix the eggs with the cream and the other ingredients, whisk and divide into 4 ramekins.

Put the ramekins in the water oven, add water halfway, and cook at 140 degrees F for 40 minutes.

Serve for breakfast right away.

Nutrition: calories 165 fat 3 fiber 8 carbs 12 protein 6

Mix Pepper Eggs

Preparation time: 10 minutes

Cooking time: 40 minutes

Servings: 4

Ingredients:

1 red onion, chopped

8 eggs, whisked

Salt and black pepper to the taste

1 tomato, cubed

¼ teaspoon chili powder

1 tablespoon cilantro, chopped

1 tablespoon butter, melted

1 red bell pepper, chopped

1 green bell pepper, chopped

Directions:

Heat up a pan with the butter over medium heat, add the onion, pepper and the other ingredients except the eggs, toss, cook for 10 minutes and take off the heat.

In a bowl, mix the eggs with salt, pepper and the sautéed ingredients and whisk.

Pour this mix into a Ziplock bag, seal, submerge in the preheated water oven and cook at 167 degrees F for 30 minutes.

Divide between plates and serve for breakfast.

Nutrition: calories 250 fat 12 fiber 5 carbs 12 protein 7

Sausage Ramekins

Preparation time: 10 minutes

Cooking time: 40 minutes

Servings: 4

Ingredients:

Salt and black pepper to the taste

1 red bell pepper, chopped

2 spring onions, chopped

1 tablespoon chives, chopped

1 tablespoon parsley, chopped

½ teaspoon sweet paprika

Cooking spray

2 sausage links, chopped

6 eggs, whisked

Directions:

Grease 4 ramekins with the cooking spray and divide the eggs mixed with the sausage, pepper and the other ingredients in each.

Carefully place ramekins in the preheated water oven and cook at 170 degrees F for 40 minutes.

Serve for breakfast right away.

Nutrition: calories 240 fat 6 fiber 4 carbs 12 protein 14

Green Beans and Mushrooms with Eggs

Preparation time: 10 minutes

Cooking time: 30 minutes

Servings: 2

Ingredients:

1 red onion, chopped

½ teaspoon sweet paprika

Salt and black pepper to the taste

1 tablespoon avocado oil, melted

4 eggs, whisked

1 cup green beans, chopped

½ cup mushrooms, sliced

Directions:

Heat up a pan with the oil over medium heat, add the onion, mushrooms and the other ingredients except the eggs, toss and sauté for 5 minutes.

In a bowl, mix eggs with sautéed mushroom mix and whisk.

Pour this into a sous vide bag, seal, submerge in the water oven and cook at 167 degrees F for 25 minutes.

Divide between plates and serve for breakfast.

Nutrition: calories 260 fat 13 fiber 6 carbs 15 protein 8

LUNCH

Bacon & Nut Stuffed Turkey Wrapped In Ham

Preparation Time: 3 hours 45 minutes

Cooking Time: 25-75 minutes

Servings: 6

Ingredients:

1 white onion, chopped

3 tbsp butter

1 cup bacon cubes

4 tbsp pine nuts

2 tbsp chopped thyme

4 garlic cloves, minced

Zest of 2 lemons

4 tbsp chopped parsley

¾ cup bread crumbs

1 egg, beaten

4 lb. boneless turkey breast, butterflied

Salt and black pepper to taste

16 slices ham

Directions:

Prepare a water bath and place the Sous Vide in it. Set to 146 F.

Heat 2 tbsp of the butter in a skillet over medium heat and sauté the onion for 10 minutes until softened. Set aside. To the same skillet, add the bacon and cook for 5 minutes until brown. Stir in the pine nuts, thyme, garlic and lemon zest and cook for 2 minutes more. Add the parsley and mix. Return the onion to the skillet, add in bread crumbs and egg and stir well.

Take out the turkey and cover it with plastic wrap. With a meat hammer pound, it to the thickness. Place the ham in an aluminum foil. Put the turkey on the ham and smash the center to create a strip. Roll the turkey tightly from one side to other until is completely wrapped. Cover the wrapped turkey with plastic wrap and place it in a vacuum-sealable bag. Release air by the water displacement method, seal and submerge the bag in the water bath. Cook for 3 hours.

Once the timer has stopped, remove the turkey and discard the plastic. Heat the remaining butter in a skillet over medium heat and put the breast. Sear the ham for 45 seconds per side. Roll the turkey and sear for 2-3 minutes more. Cut the breast into medallions and serve.

Nutrition: Calories 352, Fat 5, Fiber 3, Carbs 7, Protein 5

Caesar Salad Tortilla Rolls With Turkey

Preparation Time: 1 hour 40 minutes

Cooking Time: 25-75 minutes

Servings: 4

Ingredients:

2 garlic cloves, minced

2 skinless, boneless turkey breasts

Salt and black pepper to taste

1 cup mayonnaise

2 tbsp freshly squeezed lemon juice

1 tsp anchovy paste

1 tsp Dijon mustard

1 tsp soy sauce

4 cups iceberg lettuce

4 tortillas

Directions:

Prepare a water bath and place the Sous Vide in it. Set to 152 F. Season the turkey breast with salt and pepper and put it in a vacuum-sealable bag. Release air by the water displacement method, seal and submerge the bag in the water bath. Cook for 1 hour and 30 minutes.

Combine the mayonnaise, garlic, lemon juice, anchovy paste, mustard, soy sauce and remaining salt and pepper. Allow to rest in the fridge. Once the timer has stopped, remove the turkey and pat dry. Slice the turkey. Mix the lettuce with the cold dressing. Pour one-quarter of the turkey mixture into each tortilla and fold. Cut by the half and serve with the dressing.

Nutrition: Calories 352, Fat 5, Fiber 3, Carbs 7, Protein 5

Sage Turkey Roulade

Preparation Time: 5 hours 15 minutes

Cooking Time: 25-75 minutes

Servings: 6

Ingredients:

- 3 tbsp olive oil
- 2 small yellow onions, diced
- 2 stalks celery, diced
- 3 tbsp ground sage
- 2 lemons' zest and juice
- 3 cups turkey stuffing mix
- 2 cups turkey or chicken stock
- 5 pounds halved turkey breast

Directions:

Place a pan over medium heat, add olive oil, onion, and celery. Sauté for 2 minutes. Add the lemon juice, zest, and sage until the lemon juice reduces.

In a bowl, pour the stuffing mixture and add the cooked sage mixture. Mix it with your hands. Add in the stock gently, while mixing with your hand until ingredients hold together well and are not runny. Gently remove the turkey meat skin and lay it on a plastic wrap. Remove bones and discard.

Place the turkey breast on the skin and lay a second layer of plastic wrap on the turkey breast. Flatten it to 1 - inch of thickness using a rolling pin. Remove the plastic wrap on top and spread the stuffing on the flattened turkey, leaving ½ inch space around the edges.

Starting at the narrow side, roll the turkey like a pastry roll and drape the extra skin on the turkey. Secure the roll with butcher's twine. Wrap the turkey roll in the broader plastic wrap and twist the ends to secure the roll, which should form a tight cylinder.

Place the roll in a vacuum-sealable bag, release air and seal the bag. Refrigerate it for 40 minutes. Make a water bath, place Sous Vide in it, and set to 155 F. Place the turkey roll in the water bath and set the timer for 4 hours.

Once the timer has stopped, remove the bag and unseal it. Preheat an oven to 400 F, remove the plastic wrap from the turkey and place it on a baking dish with skin side up. Roast for 15 minutes. Slice in rounds. Serve with a creamy sauce and steamed low carb vegetables.

Nutrition: Calories 352, Fat 5, Fiber 3, Carbs 7, Protein 5

Thyme Turkey Breast

Preparation Time: 3 hours 15 minutes

Cooking Time: 25-75 minutes

Servings: 6

Ingredients:

1 turkey breast half, boneless with skin on
1 tbsp olive oil
1 tbsp garlic salt
1 tbsp thyme
1 tsp black pepper

Directions:

Prepare a water bath and place the Sous Vide in it. Set to 146 F.

Combine the turkey breast, garlic, thyme, salt and pepper. Place it in a vacuum-sealable bag. Release air by the water displacement method, seal and submerge the bag in the water bath. Cook for 4 hours.

Once the timer has stopped, remove the bag and pat dry with a baking sheet. Heat an iron skillet over high heat and sear for 5 minutes until golden.

Nutrition: Calories 352, Fat 5, Fiber 3, Carbs 7, Protein 5

DINNER

Foie Gras

Preparation Time: 10 mins

Cooking Time: 20 mins

Servings: 4

Ingredients:

Foie gras, cut into 1¼-inch pieces across lobe *

Sea salt, to taste

Directions:

Attach the sous vide immersion circulator using an adjustable clamp to a Cambro container or pot filled with water and preheat to 137°F.

Into a cooking pouch, add foie gras. Seal pouch tightly after squeezing out the excess air. Place pouch in sous vide bath and set the cooking time for 15-20 minutes.

Remove pouch from sous vide bath and carefully open it. Remove foie gras from pouch. With paper towels, pat foie gras completely dry.

Season with salt and serve immediately.

Nutrition: Calories 317 Total Fat 10.6g Total Carb 0.5g Dietary Fiber 0.2g Protein 52.1g

Frog legs with risotto

Preparation Time: 25 mins

Cooking Time: 45 mins

Servings: 4

Ingredients:

For Frogs Legs:

4 pounds frog legs

½ cup plus 3 tablespoons butter, divided

5 chicken broth ice cubes

5 fresh thyme sprigs

8 garlic cloves, minced

2 lemon slices

1 bay leaf

½ teaspoon red pepper flakes, crushed

kosher salt and freshly ground black pepper, to taste

3 tablespoons grape seed oil

For Risotto:

4-6 cups vegetable broth

15 ounces pure, unsweetened carrot juice

3 tablespoons grapeseed oil

1½ cups Vialone Nano risotto

1 medium onion, minced

1 cup chardonnay white wine

1 cup bagged frozen carrot/pea mix

½ cup mascarpone cheese

Directions:

Attach the sous vide immersion circulator using an adjustable clamp to a Cambro container or pot filled with water and preheat to 135°F.

With a sharp knife, cut between the doubled frog legs to separate into two.

Into a cooking pouch, add frog leg pieces, ½ cup of butter, thyme, garlic, bay leaf, red pepper flakes, salt and black pepper. Seal pouch tightly after squeezing out the excess air. Place pouch in sous vide bath and set the cooking time for 45 minutes.

Remove pouch from sous vide bath and carefully open it. Remove frog pieces from pouch. With paper towels, pat frog pieces completely dry.

In a large sauté pan, heat oil and remaining butter over medium-high heat, and sear frog pieces until browned slightly.

Meanwhile for risotto:

In a pan, add broth and carrot juice and bring to a boil. Reduce heat to low and allow to simmer.

- In a large heavy-bottomed pan, heat oil over medium heat and sauté risotto rice and onion for 2 minutes.
- Add wine and cook until absorbed, stirring continuously.
- Add hot broth mixture ½ cup at a time, and cook until absorbed, stirring continuously. (This process will take 15 minutes.)
- Add carrots/peas and cook for 3 minutes, stirring continuously.
- Remove from heat and stir in mascarpone cheese, salt and black pepper.
- Divide risotto onto serving plates. Top with frog meat and serve immediately.

Nutrition: Calories 317 Total Fat 10.6g Total Carb 0.5g Dietary Fiber 0.2g Protein 52.1g

Oxtail Over Vegetable Mash

Preparation Time: 15 mins

Cooking Time: 21 Hour 15 mins

Servings: 4

Ingredients:

For Oxtail:

8 medium whole onions, unpeeled

1 full garlic bulb, unpeeled

1 cup white wine

½ cup Demerara sugar

⅛ teaspoon ground cloves

pinch of cayenne pepper

salt and freshly cracked black pepper, to taste

4 pounds oxtail pieces

For Sauce:

2 tablespoons butter

4 medium carrots, peeled and cut into half-moons

2 celery sticks, finely chopped

1 medium leek, thinly sliced

10 closed cup mushrooms, thinly sliced

2 teaspoons English mustard

3 cups cooking liquid from oxtail

4 tablespoons onion puree from oxtail

pinch of cayenne pepper

salt and freshly cracked black pepper, to taste

Directions:

Preheat oven to 392°F and line a baking sheet with a piece of foil.

Arrange onions and garlic bulb onto prepared baking sheet.

Roast for 50 minutes. After 15 minutes, remove garlic bulb from oven and keep aside.

Remove onions from oven and keep aside with garlic to cool completely.

After cooling, squeeze onion pulp and garlic pulp from the skins and retain.

Into a small pan, add wine, sugar, cloves, cayenne pepper, salt, black pepper, onion and garlic pulp and bring to a boil. Simmer for 10-15 minutes.

With an immersion blender, blend the onion mixture into a thick paste. Remove from heat and keep aside cool completely.

Attach the sous vide immersion circulator using an adjustable clamp to a Cambro container or pot filled with water and preheat to 180°F.

Into a cooking pouch, add oxtail pieces and onion puree and freeze for 15 minutes.

Remove from freezer and seal pouch tightly after squeezing out the excess air. Place pouch in sous vide bath and set the cooking time for 20 hours.

Remove pouch from sous vide bath and carefully open it. Remove oxtail pieces from pouch.

Through a sieve, strain cooking liquid into a bowl and refrigerate to cool. (Reserve 4 tablespoons of this onion puree separately for the sauce.)

After cooling, remove solid Fat from top.

Remove meat from bones and, using 2 forks, shred. Remove any large chunks of Fat.

For sauce:

in a large pan, melt butter and sauté carrots, celery and leek until tender.

Add oxtail meat, mustard, cooking liquid, and onion puree, and bring to a boil.

Reduce heat and simmer, covered, for 10-15 minutes.

Add mushrooms and simmer for 5 minutes.

Stir in cayenne pepper, salt and black pepper, and remove from heat.

This oxtail mixture is great served over mashed potatoes.

Nutrition: Calories 317 Total Fat 10.6g Total Carb 0.5g Dietary Fiber 0.2g Protein 52.1g

Bison Rump Roast

Preparation Time: 15 mins

Cooking Time: 14 hours

Servings: 4

Ingredients:

1 x 2-pound, 2-inch thick bison rump roast
2 teaspoons dry steak rub (your choice)

Directions:

Attach the sous vide immersion circulator using an adjustable clamp to a Cambro container or pot filled with water and preheat to 130°F.

Rub bison roast with steak rub evenly.

Into a cooking pouch, add bison roast. Seal pouch tightly after squeezing out the excess air. Place pouch in sous vide bath and set the cooking time for 12-14 hours.

Remove pouch from sous vide bath and carefully open it. Remove bison roast from pouch, reserving some liquid. With paper towels, pat bison roast completely dry.

Heat a cast iron grill pan over high heat, and sear bison roast for 1 minute per side.

Remove bison roast from pan and keep aside for 5-10 minutes to rest.

Cut into thin slices and serve immediately with reserved cooking liquid.

Nutrition: Calories 317 Total Fat 10.6g Total Carb 0.5g Dietary Fiber 0.2g Protein 52.1g

Venison Loin with Hazelnut Coffee Maple Butter

Preparation Time: 15 mins

Cooking Time: 2 hours

Servings: 4

Ingredients:

For Venison Loin:

1-2-pound venison loin

3 garlic cloves, thinly sliced

kosher salt, to taste

freshly ground black pepper, to taste

1 tablespoon cumin seeds

butter or Fat of choice, as required

For Hazelnut Coffee Maple Butter:

¼ cup unsalted butter, chopped

1½ tablespoons cool hazelnut coffee

1 tablespoon maple syrup

Directions:

Attach the sous vide immersion circulator using an adjustable clamp to a Cambro container or pot filled with water and preheat to 140°F.

Coat venison loin generously with cumin seeds, salt and black pepper. Place garlic slices over loin.

Into a cooking pouch, add venison loin. Seal pouch tightly after squeezing out the excess air. Place pouch in sous vide bath and set the cooking time for 2 hours.

Into a small food processor, add butter, hazelnut coffee and maple syrup, and pulse until well-combined.

Transfer butter mixture onto a wax paper and roll into a cylinder. Refrigerate for at least 1 hour.

Remove from the refrigerator and keep aside to come to room temperature. Cut into slices.

Remove pouch from sous vide bath and carefully open it. Remove venison loin from pouch. With paper towels, pat venison loin completely dry.

In a cast iron skillet, melt butter over medium-high heat, and sear venison loin for 30 seconds per side or until golden brown.

Season with salt and pepper, and transfer onto a cutting board.

Cut into medallions. Top with coffee butter and serve.

Nutrition: Calories 317 Total Fat 10.6g Total Carb 0.5g Dietary Fiber 0.2g Protein 52.1g

Venison Shoulder

Preparation Time: 15 mins

Cooking Time: 8 hours 15 mins

Servings: 4

Ingredients:

Farmed venison bolar roast *
Salt and freshly ground black pepper, to taste
Clarified butter *
Red wine *
Cold butter, cut into small pieces *

Directions:

Attach the sous vide immersion circulator using an adjustable clamp to a Cambro container or pot filled with water and preheat to 130°F.

Season roast evenly with salt and black pepper.

Into a cooking pouch, add roast. Seal pouch tightly after squeezing out the excess air. Place pouch in sous vide bath and set the cooking time for 8 hours.

Remove pouch from sous vide bath and carefully open it. Remove venison loin from pouch, reserving pouch juices. With paper towels, pat roast completely dry.

In a skillet, melt clarified butter over a very high heat, and sear roast for 1 minute per side.

Remove from skillet and transfer onto a cutting board to rest. Cover roast with a piece of foil to keep warm.

Add reserved juices into a small pan and bring to a boil.

To the skillet used for the roast, add red wine and, using a wooden spatula, scrape the browned pieces from bottom and sides.

Strain reserved juices from the sous vide pouch into pan and bring to a boil. Cook until sauce is cooked to taste.

Reduce heat to very low. Add cold butter and cook until mixture becomes slightly thick, beating continuously.

Cut roast into slices across the grain. Serve roast slices with butter sauce.

Nutrition: Calories 317 Total Fat 10.6g Total Carb 0.5g Dietary Fiber 0.2g Protein 52.1g

Venison Burgers

Preparation Time: 20 mins

Cooking Time: 4 hours

Servings: 4

Ingredients:

1½ pound ground venison
½ pound high quality ground smoked bacon
6 ounces beer
salt and freshly ground black pepper, to taste
cooking oil, as required
4 artisan hamburger buns, as required
toppings and condiments of your choice

Directions:

Attach the sous vide immersion circulator using an adjustable clamp to a Cambro container or pot filled with water and preheat to 140°F.

Into a large bowl, add ground venison, ground bacon, beer, salt and black pepper, and gently mix until well-combined.

Make 4 patties, using ½ pound of mixture each time.

In cooking pouches, gently place the patties. Seal pouch tightly after squeezing out the excess air. Place pouch in sous vide bath and set the cooking time for 1-4 hours, depending on how well done you prefer burgers.

Remove pouches from sous vide bath and carefully open them. Remove patties from pouches. With paper towels, pat patties completely dry.

Season patties with a little salt and black pepper.

In a cast iron skillet, heat oil over high heat, and sear burgers for 45 seconds per side.

Place 1 patty in each burger and serve with your desired topping and condiments.

Nutrition: Calories 317 Total Fat 10.6g Total Carb 0.5g Dietary Fiber 0.2g Protein 52.1g

MEAT

Siu-Style Chinese Baby Back Ribs

Preparation Time: 30 minutes

Cooking Time: 4 hours

Servings: 6

Ingredients:

1/3 cup hoisin sauce

1/3 cup dark soy sauce

1/3 cup granulated sugar

3 tablespoons honey

3 tablespoons sherry vinegar

1 tablespoon fermented bean paste

2 teaspoons sesame oil

2 crushed garlic cloves

1-inch piece fresh grated ginger

1 ½ teaspoon five spice powder

½ teaspoon salt

½ teaspoon white pepper

½ teaspoon fresh ground black pepper

3 lbs. baby back ribs with the membrane removed

Cilantro leaves for garnishing

Directions:

Prepare the Sous Vide water bath using your immersion circulator and raise the temperature to 167-degrees Fahrenheit.

Take a large bowl and add the hoisin sauce, dark soy sauce, sugar, sherry vinegar, honey, bean paste, sesame oil, garlic, five spice powder, salt, ginger, white pepper, and black pepper.

Take a small-sized bowl and add 1/3 cup of the marinade, chill for later use.

Add the ribs to the remaining marinade and mix well to coat the ribs.

Divide the mixture among 3 large resealable bags and seal using the immersion method. Cook for 4 hours.

Heat up the grill to 400-degrees Fahrenheit and transfer the ribs to the grill, brush with the reserved marinade and cook for 3 minutes.

Flip them up and brush with more marinade, cook for another 3 minutes.

Transfer the dish to the cutting board and allow it to rest for 5 minutes, slice the rack into ribs and garnish with cilantro leaves. Serve!

Nutrition: Calories 334, Fat 33, Fiber 3, Carbs 14, Protein 7

Lamb And Cucumber Mix

Preparation Time: 10 minutes

Cooking Time: 1 hour and 30 minutes

Servings: 4

Ingredients:

- 2 pounds lamb stew meat, roughly cubed
- 2 tablespoons olive oil
- 1 cup cucumbers, cubed
- 1 teaspoon cumin, ground
- ¼ cup beef stock
- 4 garlic cloves, minced
- A pinch of salt and black pepper
- 1 tablespoon cilantro, chopped

Directions:

In a large sous vide bag mix the lamb with the oil, cucumber and the other Ingredients, seal the bag, cook in the water oven at 180 degrees F for 1 hour and 30 minutes, divide the mix between plates and serve.

Nutrition: Calories 244, Fat 12, Fiber 2, Carbs 5, Protein 16

Ground Lamb And Carrots Mix

Preparation Time: 10 minutes

Cooking Time: 1 hour

Servings: 4

Ingredients:

2 pounds lamb stew meat, ground

1 tablespoon balsamic vinegar

1 red onion, sliced

2 tablespoons olive oil

3 carrots, peeled and grated

1 parsnip, peeled and sliced

¼ cup red wine

1 tablespoon chives, chopped

A pinch of salt and black pepper

Directions:

In a large sous vide bag, mix the lamb with the vinegar, onion and the other Ingredients, seal the bag, submerge in the water oven, cook at 175 degrees F for 1 hour, divide the mix into bowls and serve.

Nutrition: Calories 254, Fat 14, Fiber 3, Carbs 6, Protein 17

Lamb And Capers

Preparation Time: 10 minutes

Cooking Time: 1 hour and 10 minutes

Servings: 4

Ingredients:

2 pounds lamb stew meat, cubed

1 red onion, sliced

2 tablespoons capers, drained

Juice of 1 lemon

½ teaspoon chili pepper

1 green bell pepper, cut into strips

2 tablespoons olive oil

½ teaspoon red pepper flakes, crushed

A pinch of salt and black pepper

1 tablespoon cilantro, chopped

Directions:

In a large sous vide bag, mix the lamb with the onion, capers and the other Ingredients, seal the bag, submerge in the water bath, cook at 180 degrees F for 1 hour and 10 minutes, divide the mix between plate sand serve.

Nutrition: Calories 263, Fat 14, Fiber 3, Carbs 6, Protein 20

Beef And Spicy Zucchinis

Preparation Time: 10 minutes

Cooking Time: 1 hour and 10 minutes

Servings: 4

Ingredients:

2 pounds beef stew meat, cubed

2 zucchinis, cubed

1 teaspoon chili powder

½ teaspoon hot paprika

1 red onion, sliced

2 tablespoons avocado oil

¼ cup beef stock

A pinch of salt and black pepper

1 teaspoon cayenne pepper

1 tablespoon chives, chopped

Directions:

In a large sous vide bag, mix the beef with the zucchinis, chili powder and the other Ingredients, seal the bag, cook in the water bath at 175 degrees F for 1 hour and 10 minutes, divide mix between plates and serve.

Nutrition: Calories 283, Fat 13, Fiber 4, Carbs 6, Protein 16

Pork With Tomatoes And Potatoes

Preparation Time: 10 minutes

Cooking Time: 1 hour and 40 minutes

Servings: 4

Ingredients:

2 pounds pork stew meat, roughly cubed

1 cup cherry tomatoes, halved

½ pound gold potatoes, peeled and cut into wedges

1 teaspoon sweet paprika

Juice of 1 lime

1 red onion, chopped

2 tablespoons avocado oil

3 garlic cloves, minced

1 tablespoon chives, chopped

Directions:

In a large sous vide bag, mix the pork with the tomatoes, potatoes and the other Ingredients, seal the bag, submerge in the water bath, cook at 180 degrees F for 1 hour and 40 minutes, divide the mix between plates and serve.

Nutrition: Calories 253, Fat 14, Fiber 2, Carbs 6, Protein 18

Lamb And Savoy Cabbage Mix

Preparation Time: 10 minutes

Cooking Time: 1 hour and 20 minutes

Servings: 4

Ingredients:

2 pounds lamb shoulder, cubed

2 tablespoons olive oil

1 cup Savoy cabbage, shredded

1 tablespoon balsamic vinegar

2 spring onions, chopped

1 tablespoon balsamic vinegar

A pinch of salt and black pepper

Juice of 1 lime

1 tablespoon chives, chopped

Directions:

In a large sous vide bag, mix the lamb with the cabbage, oil and the other Ingredients, seal the bag, submerge in the water bath, cook at 180 degrees F for 1 hour and 20 minutes, divide everything between plates and serve.

Nutrition: Calories 264, Fat 14, Fiber 3, Carbs 6, Protein 17

Beef With Carrots And Cabbage

Preparation Time: 10 minutes

Cooking Time: 1 hour and 30 minutes

Servings: 4

Ingredients:

2 tablespoons olive oil

2 carrots, peeled and sliced

1 cup red cabbage, shredded

Juice of 1 lime

2 tablespoons balsamic vinegar

2 pounds beef stew meat, roughly cubed

1 red onion, chopped

A pinch of salt and black pepper

½ teaspoon cumin, ground

1 tablespoon chives, chopped

Directions:

In a sous vide bag, mix the beef with the oil, carrots and the other Ingredients, seal the bag, submerge in the water oven and cook at 186 degrees F for 1 hour and 30 minutes.

Divide the mix into bowls and serve.

Nutrition: Calories 273, Fat 13, Fiber 2, Carbs 6, Protein 15

Orange Lamb

Preparation Time: 10 minutes

Cooking Time: 1 hour

Servings: 4

Ingredients:

2 pounds lamb chops

2 tablespoons olive oil

Juice of 2 oranges

2 tablespoons orange zest, grated

½ teaspoon turmeric powder

A pinch of salt and black pepper

1 tablespoon chives, chopped

Directions:

In a large sous vide bag, mix the lamb chops with the oil, orange juice and the other Ingredients, seal the bag, submerge in the water bath, cook at 180 degrees F for 1 hour, divide between plates and serve.

Nutrition: Calories 274, Fat 14, Fiber 2, Carbs 6, Protein 16

Ginger Pork

Preparation Time: 10 minutes

Cooking Time: 1 hour and 10 minutes

Servings: 4

Ingredients:

2 pounds pork shoulder, boneless and cubed

2 spring onions, chopped

1 tablespoon ginger, grated

½ teaspoon chili powder

½ teaspoon coriander, ground

A pinch of salt and black pepper

¼ cup beef stock

1 tablespoon cilantro, chopped

Directions:

In a sous vide bag, mix the pork with the ginger, spring onions and the other Ingredients, seal the bag, submerge in the water bath, cook at 175 degrees F for 1 hour and 10 minutes, divide the mix between plates and serve with a side salad.

Nutrition: Calories 264, Fat 14, Fiber 2, Carbs 8, Protein 12

Beef And Swiss Chard

Preparation Time: 10 minutes

Cooking Time: 1 hour and 10 minutes

Servings: 4

Ingredients:

2 pounds beef stew meat, roughly cubed

2 scallions, chopped

1 cup red chard, torn

Juice of 1 lime

1 tablespoon olive oil

1 teaspoon hot paprika

½ teaspoon turmeric powder

1 tablespoon chives, chopped

A pinch of salt and black pepper

Directions:

In a large sous vide bag, mix the beef with the scallions, chard and the other Ingredients, seal the bag, submerge in the water bath, cook at 176 degrees F for 1 hour and 10 minutes, divide the mix between plates and serve with a side salad.

Nutrition: Calories 200, Fat 9, Fiber 2, Carbs 6, Protein 12

Nutmeg Pork Roast

Preparation Time: 10 minutes

Cooking Time: 1 hour and 40 minutes

Servings: 4

Ingredients:

- 2 pounds pork roast, sliced
- 1 teaspoon nutmeg, ground
- Juice of ½ lemon
- ½ tablespoon lemon zest, grated
- 2 tablespoons olive oil
- A pinch of salt and black pepper
- ½ cup red wine
- 1 tablespoon chives, chopped

Directions:

In a large sous vide bag, mix the pork roast with the nutmeg, lemon juice and the other Ingredients, seal the bag, submerge in the water bath, cook at 180 degrees F for 1 hour and 40 minutes, divide roast between plates and serve with a side salad.

Nutrition: Calories 234, Fat 11, Fiber 3, Carbs 7, Protein 15

FISH & SEAFOOD

Salmon in Orange & Butter Sauce

Preparation Time: 10 minutes

Cooking Time: 30 minutes

Servings: 2

Ingredients:

For the salmon:

2 salmon steaks

Salt to taste

1 tbsp olive oil

For the butter sauce

1 cup water

1 shallot, finely chopped

1/3 cup freshly squeezed orange juice

1 tbsp lemon juice

A pinch of salt and sugar

2 tbsp butter

Directions:

Rub the fish with salt and put it into the vacuum bag together with olive oil.

Preheat the water bath to 115 degrees F.

Seal the bag and set the timer for 25 minutes.

In the meantime, cook the butter sauce.

In a small saucepan, combine water, juices, chopped shallot, salt and pepper. Bring to boil and simmer over medium heat until the amount of liquid is reduced to about 4 tbsp.

Mix in the butter, pour over the salmon and serve.

Nutrition: Calories: 409 Protein: 45 g Fats: 26g Carbs: 8 g

Oriental Soy & Ginger Fish

Preparation Time: 10 minutes

Cooking Time: 20 minutes

Servings: 2

Ingredients:

- 2 medium cod fillets
- 1/3 cup sugar free soy sauce
- 2 tbsp peanut oil
- 2 tbsp sesame oil
- 2 tbsp ginger root, grated
- 2 garlic cloves, minced

Directions:

- In a small pan, sauté ginger and garlic in peanut oil until lightly golden.
- Preheat the water bath to 135 degrees F.
- Put the fish, the sautéed ginger and garlic and the rest of the ingredients in the vacuum bag.
- Seal the bag and set the timer for 20 minutes.

Nutrition: Calories: 361 Protein: 40 g Fats: 9 g Carbs: 2 g

Cod in Hollandaise Sauce

Preparation Time: 10 minutes

Cooking Time: 20 minutes

Servings: 2

Ingredients:

- 2 medium cod fillets
- 2 tbsp olive oil
- Salt and pepper to taste
- Sous Vide Hollandaise sauce

Directions:

- Preheat the water bath to 135 degrees F.
- Rub the cod fillets with salt and pepper and put the fish and olive oil into the vacuum bag.
- Seal the bag and set the timer for 20 minutes.
- Serve with the Sous Vide Hollandaise sauce.

Nutrition: Calories: 544 Protein: 30 g Fats: 26 g Carbs: 40 g

Lemon Cod with Garlic and Capers

Preparation Time: 30 minutes

Cooking Time: 30 minutes

Servings: 2

Ingredients:

2 medium cod fillets

2 tbsp olive oil

Salt and pepper to taste

2 tbsp lemon juice

2 tbsp marinated capers

4 garlic cloves, coarsely chopped

Directions:

Rub the cod fillets with salt, pepper and lemon juice, put the fish into the vacuum bag and set aside for 30 minutes to marinate.

Preheat the water bath to 135 degrees F.

Add the capers, olive oil and garlic cloves to the vacuum bag.

Seal the bag and set the timer for 30 minutes.

Nutrition: Calories: 170 Protein: 27 g Fats: 6 g Carbs: 2 g

Spicy Cobbler

Preparation Time: 30 minutes

Cooking Time: 30 minutes

Servings: 2

Ingredients:

2 medium cobbler fillets
2 tbsp unsalted butter, softened
2 garlic cloves, minced
1 tsp red chili paste
1 tbsp fresh lemon juice
A pinch of salt

Directions:

In a small bowl, combine the softened butter with garlic, chili paste, salt and lemon juice.

Rub the cobbler fillets with the butter mixture and set aside.

In the meantime, preheat the water bath to 145 degrees F.

Seal the bag and set the timer for 30 minutes.

Nutrition: Calories: 544 Protein: 30 g Fats: 26 g Carbs: 40 g

Blue Cheese Fish

Preparation Time: 10 minutes

Cooking Time: 20 minutes

Servings: 2

Ingredients:

2 medium fish fillets of your choice (salmon, cod, trout or other)

2 tbsp olive oil

Salt and pepper to taste

Sous Vide Blue Cheese sauce

Directions:

Preheat the water bath to 135 degrees F.

Rub the fish fillets with salt and pepper and put the fish and olive oil into the vacuum bag.

Seal the bag and set the timer for 20 minutes.

Serve with the Sous Vide Blue Cheese sauce.

Nutrition: Calories: 544 Protein: 30 g Fats: 26 g Carbs: 40 g

POULTRY

Caramelized Chicken Teriyaki

Preparation Time: 10 minutes

Cooking time: 1 hour 40 minutes

Servings: 2

Ingredients:

2 chicken fillets

1 tbsp ginger juice

3 tsp sugar

½ tsp salt

2 tbsp Japanese Sake

2 tbsp unsweetened soy sauce

Directions:

In a small bowl, mix the ginger juice with salt and 1 tsp sugar.

Rub the chicken and leave it overnight to marinate.

In the morning, carefully put the chicken into the vacuum bag and preheat your sous vide machine to 140°F.

Seal the bag removing the air as much as possible, put it into the water bath and set the cooking time for 1 hour 30 minutes.

Mix 2 tsp sugar with sake and soy sauce and boil in a small skillet or saucepan until the sauce thickens a bit.

Pour half of the sauce over the cooked chicken breasts and torch the glaze until it caramelizes.

Chop the fillets and serve over white rice, drizzling with the remaining liquid half of the sauce.

Nutrition: Calories 522, Carbohydrates 32 g, Fats 18 g, Protein 58 g

Chicken Breast with Lemon and French Herbs

Preparation Time: 10 minutes

Cooking time: 3 hours 2o minutes

Servings: 2

Ingredients:

2 chicken breast fillets

Salt and pepper to taste

1 tsp olive oil

For the sauce:

1 onion, sliced

2 garlic cloves, minced

1 tbsp olive oil

1 tbsp unsalted butter

1 cup button mushrooms, coarsely chopped

2 tbsp white wine

½ cup chicken broth

1 cup cream

Salt and pepper to taste

Directions:

Preheat your sous vide machine to 145ºF.

Carefully put the chicken breasts into the vacuum bag. Add the butter, salt, pepper and halved garlic cloves and seal the bag removing the air as much as possible.

Put it into the water bath and set the cooking time for 3 hours.

While the chicken is cooking, make the sauce.

Heat olive oil in a medium skillet, and cook the chopped onion for about 2-3 minutes.

Add the butter and minced garlic and cook for 2 more minutes.

Add the chopped mushrooms and cook at the medium heat until the liquid evaporates.

Add the white wine, cook until the liquid almost evaporates and add the chicken broth and cream.

Continue cooking until the sauce thickens, add salt and pepper if needed. Set the sauce aside.

Remove the cooked chicken from the sous vide machine and roast it in a skillet on both sides until light brown. Add the sauce and wait just till it heats to the desired temperature.

Serve with mashed potato.

Nutrition: Calories 261, Carbohydrates 12 g, Fats 9 g, Protein 33 g

Chicken Breast with Mushroom Sauce

Preparation Time: 10 minutes

Cooking time: 3 hours 20 minutes

Servings: 2

Ingredients:

2 chicken breast fillets

2 tbsp lemon juice

Salt and pepper to taste

French herbs seasoning to taste

1 tsp olive oil

1 tsp butter

Directions:

In a small saucepan, mix the olive oil with the lemon juice and the herbs and set aside for an hour to marinate.

Preheat your sous vide machine to 145°F.

Carefully put the chicken breasts into the vacuum bag and seal it removing the air as much as possible.

Put it into the water bath and set the cooking time for 3 hours.

Heat 1 tsp butter in a frying pan and sear the cooked fillets for about 1 minute on each side until golden.

Nutrition: Calories 252, Carbohydrates 16 g, Fats 8 g, Protein 29 g

Italian Chicken Marsala

Preparation Time: 10 minutes

Cooking time: 2 hours 20 minutes

Servings: 2

Ingredients:

4 chicken breast fillets, bones and skin removed

Salt and pepper to taste

1 cup all-purpose flour

1 tbsp olive oil

1-pound porcini mushrooms, chopped

1 cup dry red wine

1 cup chicken broth

3 tbsp freshly chopped parsley

Directions:

Preheat your sous vide machine to 140ºF.

Carefully put the chicken breasts sprinkled with salt and pepper into the vacuum bag, and seal it removing the air as much as possible.

Put it into the water bath and set the cooking time for 2 hours.

When the time is up, remove the chicken breasts from the bag, dry them with kitchen towels and dredge them in the flour.

Heat olive oil in cast iron skillet and brown the fillets over the medium heat until golden. Set aside.

Put the chopped mushrooms in the skillet and sauté for 5 minutes. Add the wine and chicken broth, simmer for 10 minutes.

Pour the sauce over the chicken breasts and serve sprinkled with the freshly chopped parsley.

Nutrition: Calories 304, Carbohydrates 15 g, Fats 12 g, Protein 34 g

Aromatic Chicken

Preparation Time: 20 minutes

Cooking time: 1 hour 30 minutes

Servings: 4

Ingredients:

1 cup chicken stock

1 tablespoon chili sauce

1lb. boneless chicken breasts

2 cloves garlic, minced

1 good pinch salt

1 lemon, thinly sliced

4 sprigs basil

1 tablespoon olive oil

Directions:

Combine chicken stock and chili sauce in a bowl. Add the chicken breasts and cover with a clean foil.

Marinade 45 minutes.

In the meantime, heat the Sous Vide cooker to 146°F.

Pat dry the chicken with paper towels.

Combine the garlic and salt until you have a paste. Spread the past over chicken breasts and top the chicken with lemon.

Place the chicken breasts into Sous Vide bag and add-in remaining ingredients.

Vacuum seal the bag and submerge chicken in water.

Cook the chicken 1 hour 30 minutes.

Heat grill pan to high.

Remove the chicken from the cooker and open the bag.

Arrange the lemon slices on a grill pan and top with chicken.

Grill the lemon and chicken for 3 minutes per side.

Serve.

Nutrition: Calories 300, Carbohydrates 14 g, Fats 12 g, Protein 34 g

Mediterranean Chicken

Preparation Time: 10 minutes

Cooking time: 90 minutes

Servings: 2

Ingredients:

2 chicken breast fillets
½ cup sun-dried tomatoes, packed in oil
2 tablespoons oil, from the sun-dried tomatoes
Salt and black pepper, to taste
1 sprig basil
1 tablespoon olive oil

Directions:

Preheat the Sous Vide Cooker to 140°F.

Season the chicken with salt and pepper.

Heat the olive oil in a skillet. Add chicken breasts and cook for 1 minute per side.

Transfer immediately into Sous Vide bag, and add remaining ingredients.

Vacuum seal the bag and submerge in water.

Cook the chicken 90 minutes.

Remove the bag with chicken from the Cooker.

Open the bag and transfer the chicken to a warmed plate.

Serve.

Nutrition: Calories 400, Carbohydrates 17.8 g, Fats 21.7 g, Protein 33.4 g

Duck a la Orange

Preparation Time: 20 minutes

Cooking time: 2 hours 30 minutes

Servings: 2

Ingredients:

2 5oz. duck breast fillets, skin on

1 orange, sliced

4 cloves garlic

1 shallot, chopped

4 sprigs thyme

1 teaspoon black peppercorns

1 tablespoon sherry vinegar

¼ cup red wine

2 tablespoons butter

Salt, to taste

Directions:

Preheat Sous Vide cooker to 135ºF.

Place the duck breast fillets into a Sous Vide bag.

Top the breasts with orange slices, garlic, shallot, thyme, and peppercorns.

Vacuum seal the bag and submerge in water.

Cook the breasts 2 ½ hours.

Remove the bag from a water bath. Open the bag and remove the breasts.

Heat a large skillet over medium-high heat. Sear the duck, skin side down, for 30 seconds. Place the breasts aside and keep warm.

In the same skillet, add sherry vinegar and wine. Add the bag content and bring to simmer. Simmer 5 minutes.

Stir in the butter and simmer 1 minute.

Serve the duck with prepared sauce.

Nutrition: Calories 446, Carbohydrates 15.1 g, Fats 27.4 g, Protein 34.5 g

Chicken Thighs with Herbed Rice

Preparation Time: 30 minutes

Cooking time: 4 hours

Servings: 10

Ingredients:

4 chicken thighs

2 tablespoons salt

4 cups water

1 tablespoon paprika powder

2 tablespoons vegetable oil

2 tablespoons butter

Peppers:

4 red bell peppers, seeded, quartered

3 tablespoons olive oil

1 sprig thyme

Salt, to taste

Herbed rice:

¾ cup long grain rice

2 cups water

1 teaspoon salt

1 bunch parsley, chopped

1 bunch chives, chopped

Directions:

Make the chicken; heat Sous Vide cooker to 150ºF.

In a large bowl, combine salt and water. Add the chicken thighs into a bowl and cover with a clean foil. Refrigerate 4 hours. Remove the chicken, rinse, and pat dry.

Combine the butter and paprika and top the chicken. Place the chicken into Sous vide bag and vacuum seal.

Cook in the Sous Vide cooker 4 hours.

Make the peppers; combine the peppers with olive oil, thyme, and salt in a Sous Vide Bag.

Vacuum seal the peppers and cook in Sous Vide cooker for 30 minutes at 186F.

Make the rice; vacuum the rice with water, salt, and herbs. Cook in the Sous Vide cooker 60 minutes at 203ºF.

Heat vegetable oil in a skillet. Add chicken and cook until the skin is crispy.

Remove the peppers from the bag and cook in the same skillet with chicken, for 1 minute. Spread the rice on a plate. Top with chicken and bell peppers.

Nutrition: Calories 317, Carbohydrates 14.8 g, Fats 13.5 g, Protein 34.1 g

Fried Chicken

Preparation Time: 15 minutes

Cooking time: 2 hours

Servings: 8

Ingredients:

3 lb. chicken drums

1 tablespoon fine salt

Coating:

3 cups all-purpose flour

1 tablespoon onion powder

1 teaspoon garlic powder

½ tablespoon dried basil

1 tablespoon salt

2 cup buttermilk

Directions:

Preheat Sous Vide cooker to 155°F.

Season chicken with salt.

Place the chicken drums in Sous Vide bags. Vacuum seal.

Submerge in water and cook 2 hours.

Heat 3-inches oil in a pot.

Remove the chicken from bags and pat dry.

Combine all dry breading ingredients in a large bowl. Place buttermilk in a separate bowl.

Dredge chicken drums through flour, buttermilk, and flour again.

Fry chicken in batches, until golden and crispy.

Serve warm with fresh salad and favorite sauce.

Nutrition: Calories 362, Carbohydrates 39.6 g, Fats 10 g, Protein 28.4 g

SNACKS & DESSERTS

Dill Eggplant

Preparation time: 5 minutes

Cooking time: 30 minutes

Servings: 4

Ingredients:

1 pound eggplant, roughly cubed
1 tablespoon dill, chopped
1 tablespoon olive oil
1 red onion, chopped
Juice of 1 lime
½ teaspoon coriander, ground
½ teaspoon rosemary, dried
A pinch of salt and black pepper

Directions:

In a sous vide bag, mix the eggplant with the dill, oil and the other ingredients, seal the bag and cook in the water oven at 170 degrees F for 30 minutes.

Divide the mix between plates and serve.

Nutrition: calories 230, fat 12, fiber 4, carbs 8, protein 5

Creme Anglaise

Preparation time: 20 minutes

Cooking time: 20 minutes

Servings: 2

Ingredients:

- 3 egg yolks
- ½ cup milk
- ¼ cup heavy cream
- ¼ cup sugar
- 1 teaspoon vanilla

Directions:

- Preheat the water bath to 170°F.
- Combine all ingredients in a bag. Seal and cook 20 minutes.
- Blend sauce until smooth. Transfer to refrigerator and cool completely before serving.

Nutrition: Calories 277 Total Fat 177g Total Carb 14g Dietary Fiber 0g Protein 58g

Applesauce

Preparation time: 30 minutes

Cooking time: 3 hours

Servings: 2

Ingredients:

3 apples, coarsely chopped

1 cinnamon stick

Directions:

Preheat the water bath to 170°F.

Seal all ingredients in the bag. Cook 3 hours.

Transfer apples to a bowl. Remove cinnamon stick. Mash to your desired consistency.

Nutrition: Calories 142 Total Fat 46g Total Carb 37g Dietary Fiber 6g Protein 71g

Basil Tomato Sauce

Preparation time: 20 minutes

Cooking time: 1 hour

Servings: 2

Ingredients:

1 can (28-ounce whole tomatoes, crushed

1 onion, diced

2 cloves garlic, minced

1 tablespoon olive oil

1 bay leaf

1 sprig rosemary

½ teaspoon salt

½ teaspoon pepper

1 cup fresh basil, chopped

Cooked pasta for serving

Directions:

Preheat the water bath to 185°F.

Combine all ingredients in a bag. Seal and place in water bath. Cook 1 hour.

Remove bay leaves and rosemary sprig. Serve with cooked pasta.

Nutrition: Calories 158 Total Fat 97g Total Carb 25g Dietary Fiber 4g Protein 57g

Soy Chili Sauce

Preparation time: 5 minutes

Cooking time: 30 minutes

Servings: 1 cup. 8 servings

Ingredients:

1 cup light soy sauce

2 green chilies, chopped, seeded

¼ cup honey

1 teaspoon cumin

Directions:

Preheat Sous Vide cooker to 160F.

Combine all ingredients in Sous Vide bag.

Seal using water immersion technique.

Submerge the bag into the water bath.

Cook 30 minutes.

Remove the bag from cooker and serve sauce in a bowl.

Nutrition: Calories 35 Total Fat 1g Total Carb 18g DietarFiber 1g Protein 5g

Cheddar Cheese Sauce

Preparation Time: 10 min

Cooking Time: 20 min

Servings: 5-6

Ingredients:

5 ounces Cheddar cheese, sliced
1/5 tsp sodium citrate
1/3 cup water

Directions:

Set your cooking device to 167 degrees F.
Carefully place the ingredients into the vacuum bag, seal the bag and cook in the preheated water bath for 20 minutes.
When the time is up, pour the sauce into a bowl and blend with an immersion blender until even.

Nutrition: Calories: 80 Protein: 3 g Fats: 5 g Carbs: 4 g

Blue Cheese Sauce

Preparation Time: 10 min

Cooking Time: 20 min

Servings: 5-6

Ingredients:

5 ounces blue cheese, crumbled

1/5 tsp sodium citrate

1/3 cup water

Directions:

Set your cooking device to 167 degrees F.

Carefully place the ingredients into the vacuum bag, seal the bag and cook in the preheated water bath for 20 minutes.

When the time is up, pour the sauce into a bowl and blend with an immersion blender until even.

Nutrition: Calories: 73 Protein: 2 g Fats: 6 g Carbs: 2 g

CPSIA information can be obtained
at www.ICGtesting.com
Printed in the USA
BVHW082330310521
608489BV00015B/2496

9 781803 0405